# ARTISTIC
# JAPAN

## 300 Traditional Spot Illustrations

**DOVER PUBLICATIONS, INC.**
Mineola, New York

**Planet Friendly Publishing**
✔ Made in the United States
✔ Printed on Recycled Paper
   Text: 10%    Cover: 10%
Learn more: www.greenedition.org

GREEN EDITION

At Dover Publications we're committed to producing books in an earth-friendly manner and to helping our customers make greener choices.

Manufacturing books in the United States ensures compliance with strict environmental laws and eliminates the need for international freight shipping, a major contributor to global air pollution.

And printing on recycled paper helps minimize our consumption of trees, water and fossil fuels. The text of *Artistic Japan* was printed on paper made with 10% post-consumer waste, and the cover was printed on paper made with 10% post-consumer waste. According to Environmental Defense's Paper Calculator, by using this innovative paper instead of conventional papers, we achieved the following environmental benefits:

Trees Saved: 6  •  Air Emissions Eliminated: 540 pounds
Water Saved: 2,601 gallons  •  Solid Waste Eliminated: 158 pounds

For more information on our environmental practices, please visit us online at www.doverpublications.com/green

*Copyright*

*Bibliographical Note*

This Dover edition, first published in 2009, contains a new selection of images from *Artistic Japan*, a multi-volume set collected by S. Bing, originally published by Sampson Low, Marston, Searle & Rivington, Ltd., London, ca. 1888–1891. A CD-ROM containing all of the images has been included.

DOVER *Pictorial Archive* SERIES

This book belongs to the Dover Pictorial Archive Series. You may use the designs and illustrations for graphics and crafts applications, free and without special permission, provided that you include no more than ten in the same publication or project. (For permission for additional use, please write to Permissions Department, Dover Publications, Inc., 31 East 2nd Street, Mineola, N.Y. 11501.)

However, republication or reproduction of any illustration by any other graphic service, whether it be in a book or in any other design resource, is strictly prohibited.

*Library of Congress Cataloging-in-Publication Data*

Bing, Siegfried, 1838–1905.
   [Artistic Japan. Selections]
   Artistic Japan : 300 traditional spot illustrations. — Dover ed.
      p. cm.
   Originally published: London : Sampson Low, Marston, Searle & Rivington, ca. 1888–1891.
   ISBN-13: 978-0-486-46777-1
   ISBN-10: 0-486-46777-5
   1. Decoration and ornament—Japan. I. Title.

NK1484.A1B532 2009
709.52—dc22
                                                      2009010564

DESIGN BY QUADRUM SOLUTIONS LTD.

Manufactured in the United States by Courier Corporation
46777501
www.doverpublications.com

Inspired by traditional Japanese art, this elegant treasury of designs and motifs includes an array of blossoms, birds, landscapes, geishas, and samurai. The stunning black-and-white illustrations have been duplicated, combined, and artistically arranged to offer designers a wide range of creative possibilities.

Culled from *Artistic Japan,* a late-nineteenth-century periodical originally published in London, this exquisite collection features the finest examples of Japanese *objets d'art.* The accompanying CD-ROM contains high-resolution JPEG files of each page spread—exactly as shown in the book—and both high- and low-resolution grayscale JPEG files of each individual motif.

The "Images" folder on the CD contains three different folders. All of the high-resolution JPEG files of the page spreads have been placed in one folder, as have all of the high-resolution grayscale files, and the Internet-ready grayscale files. Every image has a unique file name in the following format: xxx.JPG. The first 3 digits of the file name, before the period, correspond to the number printed under the image in the book. The last 3 letters of the file name "JPG," refer to the file format. So, 001.JPG would be the first file in the folder.

Also included on the CD-ROM is Dover Design Manager, a simple graphics editing program for Windows that will allow you to view, print, crop, and rotate the images.

For technical support, contact:
Telephone: 1 (617) 249-0245
Fax: 1 (617) 249-0245
Email: dover@artimaging.com
Internet: http://**www.dovertechsupport.com**
The fastest way to receive technical support is via email or the Internet.

004

005

006

017

018

019

026

027

029

028

030

031

032

040

041

鈴木春信画

042

043

044

045

046

047

048

053

052

058

059

060

064

065

066

067

068

069

070

072

073

074

075

076

081

080

082

083

084

085

050

090

091

102

103

104

106

107

108

109

110

111

難波屋おきた

哥麿 画

115

127

128

135

136

137

138

139

140

144

143

145

146

148

147

149

150

151

152

153

154

155

158

159

160

161

162

164

165

183

182

195

196

200

201

202

077

209

215

214

213

217

218

226

227

228

231

232

233

231

234

235

236

237

238

239

245

248

247

256

258

257

259

260

261

266

144

265

267

268

269

272

271

273

277

278

279

280

281

282

283

284

285

067

289

290

291

292

293

294

295

300

301